Dedicated to all the members of D180 Fitness, past and present. Thank you for trusting me, investing in me, and being a part of my Fitnistry.

Erica,

I'm so glad that you're a part of our fitfam! You have such an amazing heart and I hope 2015 is awesome for you!

~Foreword~

I've struggled with my level of fitness at different stages of my life, found the winning recipe for success only to slip right back into a state of gluttony and laziness. My cyclical bouts with success and failure had one common theme and it was me trying to take control and harness my cravings with my own strength. Regardless of it being a new diet or workout plan, I was reminded of one valuable lesson in my weight loss journey: God and his resurrection power needs to be applied and can be applied to every area of our lives. Not until I made the connection between my physical and spiritual sides did I begin to see long lasting change. Fifty pounds lighter and 10 years later I've applied the principals found in Eat. Pray. Live. to 100's of my clients who have struggled with weight, eating disorders, and self-esteem issues. No matter what the issue you're struggling with God is more than able and more than willing to lead you to victory! #EatPrayLive

Introduction

How to Eat Properly for the Next 10 Days.

It's important to note that the meals listed are simply suggestions or a guide. We have several people who follow the menu strictly and others who do not. Each have been successful. Eat until you're content, not in physical discomfort. If the meals listed are too much for you to stomach, decrease the portion sizes but attempt to stick to the amount of meals per day.

You should be eating every 2-3 hours for the 10 day duration while awake. Focus on eating more vegetables than fruits. If you're brave enough you can even do 100% vegetables. Stick to the daily allotment of carbs. Do not consume any more than the daily allotment.

While on the detox drink only water and attempt to consume no less than ½ gallon per day. Exercise is allowed and encouraged during the 10 days but eat before and do not exercise longer than 30 minute increments without refueling on a small portion of vegetables or fruits. After the exercise session is complete make sure to refuel as well.

If these steps are followed the average person can expect to experience a double digit weight loss (if you are at least 30 pounds overweight). To further maximize the results add a herbal cleanse https://www.advocare.com/130716102/default.aspx to the 10 day experience or immediately following the 10 days.

Day 1: Recognize Your Emotional Identity

Scripture Meditation: 1 Corinthians 10:23 "I have the right to do anything," you say--but not everything is beneficial. "I have the right to do anything"--but not everything is constructive.

Many of us who have been raised in the United States do a poor job denying our flesh. If it feels good, then we indulge-or-overindulge in whatever provides a temporary feeling of euphoria. Sex, money, drugs, and even food are vehicles used to momentarily relieve us of life's monotonous or painful experiences. In our attempts to dull our senses we taint that which was created for good. And yes, even though the use of each is permissible by law and culturally accepted, it is not always beneficial.

It took me years to realize I had an unhealthy relationship with food. I was taking something created for nourishment and energy and using it as a "remedy" for boredome, depression, or as a reward to celebrate every accomplishment.

Bored? Cookies and Cream ice cream!

Depressed? Papa Johns Pizza!

Reward? Johnny Carino's apple skillet dessert!

This lack of restraint combined with the refusal to address the underlying reasons why the local Papa John's staff had my phone number memorized left me 45 pounds heavier and dodging mirrors left and right.

Many of us can attest to having a similar relationships with food. There's no law or biblical text negating the consumption of fast foods, sweets, sugary baked goods, or sodas. However, is it beneficial to your goals and aspirations to becoming the best version of you possible?

Meditation Questions: Am I using food in my life to self-medicate or to disassociate from unwanted feelings?

Is the food that I crave leading me towards the body that I crave?

When am I most vulnerable towards overeating?

Practical Solutions: Remember that it takes your brain 20 minutes to realize when you're full-so consider using the following practices to be more attentive to your body and its true needs:

Slow down the pace while eating or eat a salad prior to the main course.

Drink a glass of water prior to eating to make sure it's actual hunger and not a simple craving or thirst.

Find a healthy item that can replace one of your "comfort foods." For example-make cajun baked sweet potatoes rather than eating french fries.

Notes

_____

_____

_____

_____

_____

_____

_____

_____

_____

_____

_____

Day 1 Diet: (Eat every 2 hours)

- 1 to 1.5 gallons of water

- 1st meal

  - o 1 grape fruit   o ¼ cup of blueberries   o 1 orange   o 1 banana   o 2 ounces of carrots

- 2nd meal

  - o 1 cup of Corn (drained) o 1 can of cannellini beans (rinsed and drained) o ½ cup minced red onion o 1 can black beans (rinsed and drained) o ¼ cup red wine vinegar o 1 cup diced avocado o ¼ cup lime juice o 1 cup diced tomatoes

- 3rd meal

  - o 1 cup of cantaloupe o 1 cup of broccoli o 1 cup of cauliflower o ½ a cup of beans o 1 small apple

- 4th meal

  - o ½ cup cranberries o ½ cup chopped almonds o ½ cup corn o 1 small apple o 2 tbsp. of fat free vinaigrette

- 5th meal

  - o 2 slices of watermelon o 2 pears o 1 banana o ½ a cup of mixed vegetables o 1 cup of greens

- 6th meal

  - o 3 cups black-eyed peas o 1 cup diced red bell pepper o ½ cup diced onion o 2 cup vegetable broth o ¼ ground red pepper o ½ teaspoon of black pepper

- 7th Meal

- o   1 cup of black beans   o 1 cup of spinach leaves   o   1 cup of squash and zucchini

- 8th Meal

  - o   Mixed Vegetable soup with 100% vegetable stock

As a teen I started experimenting with drinking alcohol as were all of my friends. Soon after that I began smoking marijuana with my buddies and little did I know my life was to change forever from that point.

Over the next few years I became more involved in the party scene and less involved in sports. At some point as a young man I became addicted to alcohol and drugs and didn't know it. The more drugs and alcohol I did the more I needed. I resorted to criminal activity to support my drug habit. By this time in my life all athletics and a healthy lifestyle were gone. Over the period of about 12 years I became extremely unhealthy in all areas of my life, not just physically but mentally and spiritually. Eventually I reached a place where I was hopeless and all alone. And that's where God stepped in.

At that point, if I didn't get help I was going to die. I had already overdosed several times on heroin and crack cocaine. On one occasion I had stopped breathing, my body shut down, and fortunately I was saved by a nearby paramedic. Upon realizing that my life was at stake I reached out for help and met a group of people who would teach me how to live my life so that I didn't have to use alcohol or drugs. They saved my life. It was during this time that I renewed my relationship with God and it was through His power and grace that I became sober and clean.

Over the next several years I learned how to live a sober life. During this time I did what is common to people in recovery, I exchanged one habit for another. In my case it was food. I eventually became much heavier than I'd ever been in my life. My weight topped out at 245 pounds. I felt fat and old and like a big blob. I didn't like how I felt or looked. I developed nagging pain in my lower back, knees, and feet. I had to have orthotics made to wear in my shoes to help with the pain.

While on a family vacation in 2010, I made the decision along with other family members to lose weight. I realized at that time that as I get older carrying all this extra weight was going to be very unhealthy and just make life difficult. I wanted a better quality of life.

When I got home from my vacation I ordered and started doing some popular home DVD workouts. I thought this would help me reach my goal. Not knowing how to properly diet I did lose weight but didn't like how I looked. All I had achieved was the "skinny-fat" look. In 2012 through a friend I was introduced to D180 Fitness. Here I met Ian Buchanan and a great group of people who were on a similar fitness journey as I. And in December 2012 Ian asked me if I would be interested in training to compete in a physique competition. I was nervous and scared and didn't know how I would get to that point but Ian assured me that he would direct me the entire way. Over the next 5 months I started learning about ideal nutrition and exercise. Slowly my body started changing and I was happy and excited with the results. I also rediscovered my love and passion for athletics and sport.

On May 25th 2013, I competed in my first fitness competition against 15-20 other athletes in the Men's Physique category. As I stood on stage I couldn't help but smile. I didn't care what the judges thought or even what the audience was thinking. I didn't even care that I didn't receive a trophy. I couldn't help smiling because here I was an ex-alcoholic, heroin and crack cocaine addict now standing in front of hundreds as a picture of health. What an amazing God we serve!!!

My journey to physical fitness has been very similar to my recovery journey. When I follow the direction from good experienced people and trust the process my goals are reached. God is still in the miracle business! He has created us as spiritual and physical beings and putting the effort in to improve myself makes me more fit to do his work.

Robert Flynn

Day 2: Fight the temptation to blend in and conform.

Scripture Meditation: Romans 12:2 And do not be conformed to this world, but be transformed by the renewing of your mind, so that you may prove what the will of God is, that which is good and acceptable and perfect.

One of the amazing things about humanity is that of the billions of people that make up the world no two share the same DNA, fingerprints, or even personality. In spite of the uniqueness which comprises each of us we feel compelled to blend in with societal norms, standards, and adopt what the main stream culture views as acceptable and standard as our way of living.

It's evident in our wardrobe, methods of entertainment, value system, and what we define as beauty. As Christians we are called to be transformers and not conformers to the world. It would be easy enough to compartmentalize that calling to spiritual works but we serve a holistic God who is concerned with our mind, spirit, and body. What the world defines as beauty doesn't always coincide with the most important measure of assessment; the heart. Kanye West shared, "that the prettiest people do the ugliest things" and although that's nowhere close to being concrete it does remind us that regardless of how outwardly beautiful one may seem the heart trumps any outward notion of physical perfection.

If you're attempting to lose weight and get in shape to pursue the world's image of beauty you'll never be able to grasp contentment. You're fleeing after an imaginary destination which alludes to beauty equating to happiness. Instead start within, fall in love with who God has created you to be, and nurture the traits and attributes that make you special enough to have your own set of DNA, personality, fingerprints and leave yours on the world.

Meditation Questions: Once I achieve my goal weight/look will that make me content?

When I don't feel beautiful or attractive does that open up doors for destructive behavior in my life?

In God's eyes would I be considered beautiful?

Is there another person whose opinion of myself trumps God's?

Practical Solutions: Don't wait until you reach a certain waist line or size. Make the cautious decision to love who you are right now. Imperfections, stretch marks, excess skin, weight, body fat percentage and all. The definition of beauty doesn't require the word skinny but it does require self-love.

Arrange a photo shoot this week with a reputable photographer. Don't wait till you reach your goal weight. You'll be amazed at how beautiful you truly are without losing one more pound.

Notes

_____

_____

_____

_____

_____

_____

_____

_____

_____

_____

_____

Day 2 Diet: (Eat every 2 hours)

- 1 to 1.5 gallons of water

- 1st meal

    o 1 grape fruit o ¼ cup of blueberries o 1 orange o 1 banana o 2 ounces of carrots

- 2nd meal

    o 1 cup of Corn (drained) o 1 can of cannellini beans (rinsed and drained) o ½ cup minced red onion o 1 can black beans (rinsed and drained) o ¼ cup red wine vinegar o 1 cup diced avocado o ¼ cup lime juice o 1 cup diced tomatoes

- 3rd meal

    o 1 cup of cantaloupe o 1 cup of broccoli o 1 cup of cauliflower o ½ a cup of beans o 1 small apple

- 4th meal

    o ½ cup cranberries o ½ cup chopped almonds o ½ cup corn o 1 small apple o 2 tbsp. of fat free vinaigrette

- 5th meal

    o 2 slices of watermelon o 2 pears o 1 banana o ½ a cup of mixed vegetables o 1 cup of greens

- 6th meal

    o 3 cups black-eyed peas o 1 cup diced red bell pepper o ½ cup diced onion o 2 cup vegetable broth o ¼ ground red pepper o ½ teaspoon of black pepper

- 7th Meal

- o 1 cup of black beans o 1 cup of spinach leaves o 1 cup of squash and zucchini

- 8th Meal

    - o   Mixed Vegetable soup with 100% vegetable stock

Growing up I was always involved in sports. If there was a sport to be played in our small town then I played it! When I reached high school I decided to narrow down my extra-curricular activities and focus on playing basketball, volleyball, and softball. I excelled in all three of these sports and had the support of my entire family. I can't remember the exact year but before one of my basketball games my mom pulled me aside and said, "I will give you $50 if you score 10 points in tonight's game." That night I would score only 8 points and did not receive any money. This continued throughout the rest of my sports career. I was given an expectation by my mother and was paid if I reached the goal. It slowly began to move into other aspects of my life including my weight. My mother wanted me to look a certain way, be a certain weight, perform at a certain level, and in my mind, if I did not do so then I was letting her down. My mother's opinion of me was all that I cared about and I wanted her approval.

I went to Freed-Hardeman University on a volleyball scholarship. Although my mother was not physically there, she was always in my head. I would report my stats to her after every game just waiting to hear the words of approval from her. When I came home for holidays I was analyzed and rewarded per her approval.

It was during my sophomore year of college that I began dating a guy who was a personal trainer and bodybuilder. In my mind I now had to stay even more at the top of my game because if I did not stay physically fit and thin then he would not approve and leave me. We ended up dating for 5 years and then got engaged. I was so excited and couldn't wait to go shopping for my wedding dress. My mom, my two sisters, and I all met in Nashville to go shopping. I picked out some dresses to try on and when I came out in the first dress my mom started crying. However, these were not tears of joy but rather tears of sadness and embarrassment. It was a sleeveless dress and she said that I had too much fat coming out of the top of the dress under my arms. I was devastated. I ended up getting that dress because it was the one my sisters thought I looked the best in but in my mind I knew I would never wear it in public, especially if my mom did not think I looked pretty in it. My husband and I ended up getting married at the courthouse and I sold the dress on the internet.

After three years of marriage I was devastated to find out that my husband was having an affair with another woman. I remember one conversation we had in which he told me that the reason he was with this woman was because I was too fat and too religious. Those words will forever be stuck in my head. During the divorce process I attempted suicide and was being closely monitored at all times. I could not keep any food down so naturally I had lost a lot of weight. It was the smallest I had been in a very long time and it was a weight that my mom was happy with and my ex-husband would have been happy with. However, mentally I was a disaster.

After a lot of counseling and a lot of prayers, God brought me back to a good and safe place. Although physically I had gained a lot of weight I was now in a healthy mental state. It's almost impossible to take care of yourself properly from a physical standpoint when mentally you're in turmoil. I finally desired to get to a place physically that I desired. Not for my mom. Not for my ex-husband but for myself. I heard about D180 from a friend and decided to give it a try. Today I am working with Ian and my new found family at D180 to become a healthier, happier, and more confident person. God has blessed me with a safe place for any person at any weight and I'm forever grateful. The encouragement and the 1-on-1 attention given to me is something you can't put a price on. I take life one day at a time and each day I'm getting better than the one before.

Mallory Garrett

Day 3: Relentlessly Pursue

Scripture Meditation: Proverbs 24:16 - "Even if good people fall seven times, they will get back up. But when trouble strikes the wicked, that's the end of them."

Failure is the best teacher we have at our disposal yet in still it's something we fear and avoid at all cost. We don't praise the little kid who falls time and time again in attempts to learning how to ride his bike or the student who repeats a grade due to lack of comprehension. We sweep failure under the rug. We speak about it quietly not realizing that the lessons learned through failure are preparing us to ride faster and graduate sooner; to become better, stronger, more focused versions of ourselves. Failures are to be welcomed not avoided.

Donald Trump emphatically states, "Sometimes by losing a battle you find a new way to win the war"

Some of the most influential people in history achieved momentous success prefaced by failure. Albert Einstein was unable to speak until he was almost 4 years old, Michael Jordan was cut from his high school basketball team, Oprah Winfrey was fired from a news anchor job, Walt Disney filed for bankruptcy, and Abraham Lincoln lost 8 elections on his way to being elected President of the United States.

We all fall short, stumble, and fail in life. Some failures are seemingly greater than others but regardless of a 10 foot drop or 10 inch stumble failing doesn't define you. What you do afterwards will always carry more weight. Will you get back up and continue to fight towards your goals or timidly wave the white flag of surrender? Every journey in life worth reaching comes with its share of obstacles and the road to health and wellness is no different. If you fail during a workout or following through with your diet don't allow that moment to define you but empower you! Get back up, refocus, forgive yourself, and keep pressing forward.

"It's hard to beat a man or a woman who refuses to give up." Author Unknown

Meditation Questions: In your pursuit for healthy living have there been times when you have fallen?
Have you responded to past failures correctly?

What should be the ideal response to falling during your health and fitness journey?

Practical Solutions: Create a list of 3 of your greatest successes in the last 2 years. Think about how you felt once you achieved each of those 3 accomplishments. Happy? Elated? Relieved?

Now think even further back to the steps taken to achieve those successes. Chances are the more you had to go through to obtain it the more you appreciated its obtainment. Failure simply adds power to your story.

Notes

_____

_____

_____

_____

_____

_____

_____

_____

_____

_____

_____

_____

Day 3 Diet: (Eat every 2 hours)

- 1 to 1.5 gallons of water

- 1st meal

    o 1 grape fruit   o 1 apple   o 1 orange   o 1 banana   o 2 ounces of carrots

- 2nd meal

    o ¼ cup Bell Peppers   o ¼ cup Squash   o ¼ Zucchini   o ¼ Onions

- 3rd meal

    o Kale salad   o cranberries   o chopped almonds   o corn   o 1 small apple

- 4th meal

    o Soup with 100% vegetable stock   o Carrots   o Corn   o Black Beans   o ½ a cup of brown rice

- 5th meal

    o 2 slices of watermelon   o 2 pears   o 1 banana   o ½ a cup of mixed vegetables   o 1 cup of greens

- 6th meal

    o 1 bowl of cherries   o 2 mandarins oranges   o Grapefruit   o 2 plums

- 7th Meal

    o 1 cup of black beans   o 1 cup of spinach leaves   o 1 cup of squash and zucchini

- 8th Meal

    o Mixed Vegetable soup with 100% vegetable stock

There is never a moment's rest in my mind concerning my weight. It's all I think about and all I fight against. "My goodness girl you are getting huge!" "As good as your husband looks you better lose some weight before you lose him!" Two of the many comments thrown my way. My weight literally causes pain in every area of my life, but the most traumatic is that I have allowed it to defile my marriage bed. I have been married 13 years to the man of my dreams. He is athletic, handsome, and full of life. If his stately appearance isn't enough, he spoils me rotten. He exhales voluminous praise my way; you're beautiful, sexy, gorgeous, hot, and all those other adjectives a girl loves to hear yet, I think he is lying. Why? Because I am FAT. The once high school starting point guard is now a fat, unfit, unsexy, unattractive mess.

In October 2012, I came to the realization that I was 34 years old and morbidly obese, how sad! Everyone notices this good-looking guy, ah but who is on his arm? Me, morbidly obese, me. Real talk, great sex is so important in a martial relationship. For me, there is no greater ecstasy on this earth than making love to my husband. As I have transformed into an elephant, my husband's once eager enchantress has become a dispassionate disgust. Forget the lingerie, no more wild rendezvous, no more games, and don't even think about turning those lights on buddy! My weight has stolen my sensuality and caused me to restrict my husband's access to what should be his garden of sanctification, satisfaction & delight. It's debilitating, it's crippling, it's treacherous, it's painful, it's my life. Now to top all that off, I'm a Christian and there is more guilt because I feel my faith is lacking. OMG, saved, loved, accepted, anointed, powerful but defeated...how does that work?

I am a qualifying candidate for a gastric bypass and I've considered it over and again. Surgery could offer a quick fix but I just couldn't do it. I don't judge those who choose that option, but for me, having weight loss surgery would be like receiving the crown without the fight. So, what then? One Sunday night, not long ago, I studied 1Kings 18. God announced to the prophet Elijah that he would send rain upon the earth after a 3 year famine. He told Elijah to go present himself to the king, which was his enemy, and tell the king what God promised. Elijah was obedient to God. He presented himself to his enemy the king and announced the forecast, "There is the sound of an abundance of rain." Elijah sent one of his servants to go and look for the rain. The servant went and came back and reported to Elijah that he saw nothing. Elijah told him to go again. Seven times Elijah sent his servant to go look for what God had promised, six times the man said he saw nothing. The seventh time the servant reported seeing a cloud the size of a man's hand. The rain was on the way.

My cycle of failure in the area of weight loss had caused a 13 year famine in my life. However, I realized that I could face the enemy of obesity because He who has promised is faithful. I fight the enemy of obesity, not alone, but with the promises of God. No matter how long or intense the struggle, no matter how many times you've failed...Go Again, because the rain is on the way! The rain of a healthy life style is coming! Hold on to God's promises and GET UP and GO, and GO AGAIN, and AGAIN, and AGAIN! Go workout, go ask for help, and go make better food choices and do it for as long as it takes. Starting that Sunday night & now every day, I look in the mirror and say, "I am going to get up and go until what has been promised is made manifest!"

Mrs. Ebony Shaw-Taylor

Day 4: Whatever your best is…Give it.

Scripture Meditation: Colossians 3:23 Whatever you do, work at it wholeheartedly as though you were doing it for the Lord and not merely for people.

There's something about a sale that intrigues even the most miserly consumer. A certain amount of excitement occurs when we find out our favorite store or favorite item is on sale. We will make a way despite no cash, no credit or transportation to get our hearts desires. The bottom line is that we love sales because we get the same product at a discounted price. We get the same item for half the cost of what others have paid full value.

Now in the world of consumerism that's coveted but when it comes to our relationship with God many of us attempt to get the same blessings as others at half the cost. We don't want to pay the price of reading the word, pay the price of setting aside prayer time with God, pay the price of fasting, pay the price of going to more than one Church service a week. We want to barely get by with a "50% off" attitude of serving the Savior and yet we expect the same amount of prosperity, blessings, success, peace and happiness of those who have paid the full price.

If we can so easily adopt this mindset in regards to the most significant of relationship in life it's not a stretch to recognize we can often approach our fitness journey with a "'50% off' mentality. Don't expect to see the weight loss, muscle gain, and overall transformation as others who gave 100% if you're only committed to eating, exercising, and denying your flesh 50% of the time.

There is a direct correlation between our spiritual and physical lives. The same effort, discipline, and sacrificial living that you're willing to give for God can be seen in the overall discipline and lifestyle you have in your fitness journey. The more you deny your flesh and abstain from those unhealthy but tasty items the easier it becomes to deny your flesh on the bigger issues in your life.

"It's going to hurt! There is going to be pain, sweat, and adversity. You are going to doubt yourself before you get there. You will wonder if you can do it, and you will try to talk yourself out of giving it all. You are going to see "easy ways out." All along the way you will be presented with ways to give less of yourself." (Author Unknown)

Don't.

Meditation Questions: Is there anything in your life that you are willing to give 100% effort to?

Will that entity make giving 100% to your health and fitness journey more accessible? How so?

Will a "50% off" mindset get you the figure/physique that you desire?

Practical Solutions: Approach your journey one day at a time. Sometimes focusing on the big picture can be overwhelming. Instead of fixating on a month out or even 10 days away focus your attention on today. Whatever your 100% looks like today; give it.

When exercising have a time limit cut off of 45 minutes to an hour. During that time go as intense as you possibly can and once that time is up so is your workout.

Notes

_____

_____

_____

_____

_____

_____

_____

_____

Day 4 Diet: (Eat every 2 hours)

- 1 to 1.5 gallons of water

- 1st meal

    o 1 grape fruit o 1 apple o 1 orange o 1 banana o 2 ounces of carrots

- 2nd meal

    o ¼ cup Bell Peppers o ¼ cup Squash o ¼ Zucchini o ¼ Onions

- 3rd meal

    o Kale salad o cranberries o chopped almonds o corn o 1 small apple

- 4th meal

    o Soup with 100% vegetable stock o Carrots o Corn o Black Beans o ½ a cup of brown rice

- 5th meal

    o 2 slices of watermelon o 2 pears o 1 banana o ½ a cup of mixed vegetables o 1 cup of greens

- 6th meal

    o 1 bowl of cherries o 2 mandarins oranges o Grapefruit o 2 plums

- 7th Meal

    o 1 cup of black beans o 1 cup of spinach leaves o 1 cup of squash and zucchini

- 8th Meal

    o Mixed Vegetable soup with 100% vegetable stock

I was born to a teenage mother and father who fought to overcome the negative statistics that society tends to assign to them. My parents married young and worked hard to provide a lifestyle that was much different than their own. My mother was our backbone guiding us spiritually and emotionally even when her own needs were neglected. My father encouraged high academic achievement and was pleased with the 4.3 GPA I earned in high school. I was a cheerleader and gymnast throughout school and I dreamed of becoming a doctor. I felt as if nothing could stop me. Then I met a boy and I fell in love.

I married the boy I met in high school because I was taught marriage was honorable and I had seen my parents have a successful marriage. I gave birth to two amazing little girls and had climbed my way up the corporate ladder with the company I had worked for since high school. I was ambitious, focused and driven. My husband was in the Air Force and life was good. Everything changed for me in one moment on a summer day. I received the news that the boy whose life was just beginning was cut short by a fatal car accident. Everything in my world was never the same. At the age of 23, I was instantly a widow with four eyes looking at me. It was in that moment that on the inside I died spiritually and stood emotionally still.

I felt as if I had been abandoned and left all alone. I felt as if God had left me. I was not able to allow myself to grieve so I set out on a path of self-destructive behavior. I became a functional alcoholic. I drank when I felt no one was looking because I had to wear the face of the bright eyed girl everyone was used to. I kept the company of people who meant me no good which resulted in a person I thought was my friend raping me. Abandonment and loneliness made new friends by the name of guilt and shame. They tormented me every time I looked in the mirror. My self-destructive behavior turned into complete self-rejection. I felt as if God could no longer love someone like me. I turned from drinking alcohol to food. Food felt safe and I could self-medicate out in the open. Food was my coping mechanism.

I could not see that food had become my god and had become the answer to all of my problems. I had become very functional at being dysfunctional. I had settled in my mind that this would be my life. I smiled every day and no one ever saw the pain in my eyes. I met my current husband who I was reluctant to marry due to personal fears. He was very patient with me and protective in a way I had never experienced. He made me feel complete and that sense of abandonment started to fade. I found out I was pregnant with a son. I was excited about the pregnancy but it ended at 30 weeks as a stillbirth due to diabetic complications from the weight I gained from my open addiction. I felt the presence of death in my body as I delivered my son. I carried the heavy weight of my son's death on my shoulders because I felt that I killed him……with food. I made several attempts to lose weight but failed every time because I was trying to take an outside in approach. I knew something needed to change but didn't know where to begin. For the first time in ten years I could admit I was lost. I repented and asked God to help me. I asked Him to show me how to love me.

While on vacation in Tennessee, a family member introduced me to D180 fitness. I initially looked at the program as just another fitness fad. I had told myself I would fail. I started to do the workouts online. They were tough but there was something refreshing about the program that made me want to keep going. There was support within this group. Everyone celebrates you. I was finally able to acknowledge that my emotions were attached to food and I had spiritually replaced God with food. I started to renew my mind with God's word and scriptures filled with the love He has for me. I finally found the truth of God's word: I am fearfully and wonderfully made. God does love me. He did not reject me I rejected Him. Fitness allowed to me to manage my negative emotions. The word of God showed me who I really am: someone worth far more than rubies.

Now I celebrate the company of good people rather than food. Every day is not easy and sometimes the old me tries to resurface but Christ continues to remind me ever so gently: "Therefore if any man is in Christ, he is a new creature; old things passed away; behold, new things have come." 2 Corinthians 5:17. Every weight I lift, every mile I run, every calorie I burn proves I am victorious rather than the victim. The best part for me is that this is just the beginning.

Kiana Northern

Day 5: Progress not Perfection

Scripture Meditation: 1 Timothy 4:8 For physical training is of some value, but godliness has value for all things, holding promise for both the present life and the life to come.

The Perfect Season, The Perfect Game, The Perfect Woman, The Perfect Couple. People get excited about the possibility of perfection. Because in a world filled with so much imperfection, flawed idealism, broken dreams, ill wished desires we need to be able to hold on to the idea that maybe there's something better out there, than what the world has consistently shown us. That's why we invest our time, emotions, and money into gym memberships, personal trainers, movies with happy endings, liposuction, and online dating because of our strong desire and hope that one day not only will we be able to see perfection but we will be a part of the illusive seemingly fictitious being.

The truth of the matter is that as long as you search for perfection without including Christ in the mix your search will be in vain. Matthew 5:48 mandates us, "You, therefore, must be perfect, as your heavenly Father is perfect."

In a world filled with decaying morality and in a time of nebulous values we are still expected to be like Christ...PERFECT. It doesn't mean we'll lead the perfect life but it's possible we could have a perfect hour, a perfect day, or even a perfect week and in doing so be a witness to the lost still in search of perfection.

Let's continue to represent for Christ lifting the standards around us and unveiling to the world what true Perfection has the capability of looking like. Not an external beauty that decays with the years but an internal magnificence that ceases to rust, ceases to die out, ceases to deteriorate.

For those of you seeking physical perfection you're on a journey that will yield unfulfilling results. Looks fade. Muscles atrophy. Six packs disappear.

Instead focus on the one who is able to leave you satisfied for eternity.

Meditation Questions: If a perfect Creator creates an imperfect creation is the creation imperfect or perfectly and purposely flawed? Why would God make you purposely flawed?

What is the driving force behind your health and fitness journey?

Is physical perfection a realistic goal to obtain?

Practical Solutions: Some of the most magnificent monuments in the world are flawed (Leaning Tower of Pisa and Sphinx) but draw millions of onlookers yearly. Why? Because their imperfection adds to their beauty.

Create a list of your physical imperfections.

Now explain why these are imperfections and not simply differences?

Have you been listening to God's voice in regards to your physical attributes or someone else?

Notes

_____

_____

_____

_____

_____

_____

_____

_____

_____

_____

Day 5 Diet: (Eat every 2 hours)

- 1 to 1.5 gallons of water

- 1st Meal: Mixed Fruit Bowl

  - 1 apple(diced), 1 banana (chopped), 2 mandarin oranges (peeled and separated), ¼ cup of blueberries. Mix together

- 2nd Meal:

  - 2 cups of cauliflower, 3 garlic cloves (minced), 1 tsp. smoked paprika, 1/2 tsp. chili powder, 1 tsp. turmeric, 1/4tsp. cayenne pepper. Mix, drizzle with olive oil, Bake @400 for 35mins

  - 1 apple, 1pear

- 3rd Meal:

  - 2 cups 100% vegetable stock, 1 Carrot (peeled and sliced), 1 Can of Corn (drained), 1 can of Black Beans (rinsed and drained), 2 Stocks of Celery (chopped), ½ cup of brown rice

- 4th Meal:

  - 1cup kale, 1 cup baby spinach, 1 cup shredded cabbage, 10 almonds (roughly chopped), 3 strawberries(sliced) 1 carrot (large, peeled & sliced) 1/4 cup blueberries1/3 cucumber (peeled, seeded & sliced) 1/4 cup raspberries and 2 tbsp. Fat Free Raspberry vinaigrette

- 5th Meal

  - 2 slices of watermelon o 2 pears o 1banana o ½ a cup of mixed vegetables o 1 cup of greens

- 6th Meal:

- 3 cups black-eyed peas o 1 cup diced red bell pepper o ½ cup diced onion o 2 cup vegetable broth o ¼ ground red pepper o ½ teaspoon of black pepper

- 7th Meal:

  - 1 Can Black Beans (drained), 1 Yellow Squash (diced) 1 Zucchini (diced), 1Can of Diced Tomatoes with Green Chile Peppers, ½ onion chopped, ½ tsp. garlic powder. Combine and Sautee until tender-crisp

- 8th Meal:

  - 2 cups 100% vegetable stock, 1 Carrot (peeled and sliced), 1 Can of Corn (drained), 1 can of Black Beans (rinsed and drained), 2 Stocks of Celery (chopped), ½ cup of brown rice

On March 18, 2005 I sat uncomfortably crammed into a chair with arm rests in my doctor's exam room. I was wearing a men's size 3xl Kelly green polo shirt and a size 30W jeans. My weight was out of control at over 400 pounds. My doctor spoke calmly. "These blood pressures are dangerously high. I am going to begin trying you on samples of blood pressure medicines today. I am worried. Your life is at risk."

To say that was a turning point is quite an understatement. I had no idea in that moment that I would ever be where I am now… in ONEDERLAND! This period of my life marks the first time I have stepped on the scale and seen a 1 in front of my weight since elementary school. WHAT? I know! That's right I weighed 200 pounds or more throughout my fifth grade school year. My weight only increased from there. I grew up the fat kid. Genetically predisposed to weight gain. The metabolism of a slug. And not just one sweet tooth. Oh no! I like to say ALL my teeth are sweet teeth. My favorite food? Ice cream. Second favorite? Skittles. Seriously. People usually ask when they find out I have lost about 200 pounds "How?"

I say "the good and bad news is a healthy diet and exercise." I mean good news if I can do it, YOU can do it! The bad news is YOU are the only one who can do it. No one can do it for you. But how empowering!!!! You got this!! There is hope for you!

I lost 200 pounds weight through diet and exercise, and I prayed to be free of the guilt and shame I lived under for allowing myself to be so unhealthy. Perhaps this is the most important point in my story. God began to speak to me concerning the shame. The embarrassment and guilt overshadowed any achievement. All encouragement was dismissed with no eye contact and "thanks I'm working on it" or "gosh thanks I have a long ways to go." At some point the shame and guilt turned into conviction. Conviction of my refusal to accept the life encompassing forgiveness and freedom in Christ. I had no trouble accepting forgiveness from all other past shortcomings but this struggle with food and over eating? On me. Lies! This verse remains my foundation. "There is therefore no condemnation for those who are in Christ Jesus." How freeing is that? I am no longer a slave to past habits or choices or addictions, I now walk in the hope of Christ. One success led to another. It was never easy. I had to make major life changes to stay on track. Each day now is a conscience choice to do the things that bring me closer to the person I was created to be.

My advice is this. Treat your workout like you treat brushing your teeth. You do not debate whether or not you will do it each day. Do it. No excuses. Period. Find a balanced nutrition plan that works for you and stick to it. Surround yourself with people on a journey similar to yours. And the biggest thing is don't be afraid to bring this journey to God. He is not only concerned about our spiritual well-being. He wants us to physically live victoriously and he cares about this! He cares about you!

Amber Kail

Day 6: Relentlessly Pursue

Scripture: 2 Timothy 4:7 I have fought the fight, I have ran the race, I have kept the faith.

We live in a world that is unapologetically drawn to instant gratification. A world that encourages and even applauds cutting corners and skipping steps to obtain what the heart desires. The problem with instant gratification is that it does a tremendous disservice to the value and life lessons learned through failure, through rejection, and through tenaciously pursuing whatever has occupied your longings. Instant gratification cheapens the journey while focusing solely on the final destination. It doesn't allow us time to celebrate the small accomplishments because no matter how much incremental success we obtain it will always pale in comparison to the desired final result.

There is value in obtaining what your heart seeks but even more value in appreciating and welcoming the necessary steps for achievement. In regards to pursuing and attaining your health and fitness goals you're faced with an important question. What method of payment are you going to use: Tenaciously pursuing your goals through hard work and sacrifice or skipping as many steps as possible in hopes of reaching the finish line faster? You don't have to answer verbally. Your actions have and continue to shout the truthful response.

Those who travel the long and lonely road of hard work, discipline, sweat, and tears have a greater sense of appreciation once their goals are obtained. They realize that a monetary value can't be placed on what they've earned because through the struggle, the pain, and the disappointments linked to the journey, God takes the opportunity to reveal how truly strong, beautiful, and perfectly imperfect he has created you to be.

The greatest lessons learned take place during the race, not at the finish line.

Meditation Questions: Have I decided which method of payment I'm willing to use to obtain a healthy and fit lifestyle?

If my journey takes twice as long as desired will it lessen or increase my appreciation once attained?

Practical Solutions: Celebrate the smaller accomplishments. Have you lost 5 pounds, 10 pounds lately? Time to celebrate! Following the 10th day of this journey treat yourself to your favorite restaurant and acknowledge how proud you should be of this accomplishment!

Create a timeline of your results starting with you at your heaviest and track the progress you've made up unto this day. Continue to track your progress and use your start as a reminder of how far you've come.

Notes

_____

_____

_____

_____

_____

_____

_____

_____

_____

_____

_____

Day 6 Diet: (Eat every 2 hours)

- 1 to 1.5 gallons of water

- 1st Meal:

    o 1 apple (diced), 1 banana (chopped), 2 mandarin oranges (peeled and separated), ¼ cup of blueberries. Mix together

- 2nd Meal:

    o 2 cups of cauliflower, 3 garlic cloves (minced), 1 tsp. smoked paprika, 1/2 tsp. chili powder, 1 tsp. turmeric, 1/4tsp. cayenne pepper. Mix, drizzle with olive oil, Bake @400 for 35mins

    o 1 apple, 1pear

- 3rd Meal:

    o 2 cups 100% vegetable stock, 1 Carrot (peeled and sliced), 1 Can of Corn (drained), 1 can of Black Beans (rinsed and drained), 2 Stocks of Celery (chopped), ½ cup of brown rice

- 4th Meal:

    o 1cup kale, 1 cup baby spinach, 1 cup shredded cabbage, 10 almonds (roughly chopped), 3 strawberries(sliced) 1 carrot (large, peeled & sliced) 1/4 cup blueberries1/3 cucumber (peeled, seeded & sliced) 1/4 cup raspberries and 2 tbsp. Fat Free Raspberry vinaigrette

- 5th Meal

    o 2 slices of watermelon o 2 pears o 1banana o ½ a cup of mixed vegetables o 1 cup of greens

- 6th Meal:

- o 3 cups black-eyed peas o 1 cup diced red bell pepper o ½ cup diced onion o 2 cup vegetable broth o ¼ ground red pepper o ½ teaspoon of black pepper

- 7th Meal:

  - o 1 Can Black Beans (drained), 1 Yellow Squash (diced) 1 Zucchini (diced), 1Can of Diced Tomatoes with Green Chile Peppers, ½ onion chopped, ½ tsp. garlic powder. Combine and Sautee until tender-crisp

- 8th Meal:

  - o 2 cups 100% vegetable stock, 1 Carrot (peeled and sliced), 1 Can of Corn (drained), 1 can of Black Beans (rinsed and drained), 2 Stocks of Celery (chopped), ½ cup of brown rice

My grandmother worked as a housekeeper and nanny for a family who had a college-aged daughter. She would always pass down her Cosmopolitan magazines to me after she read them. So when I was 15 one of the issues of Cosmo had a weight chart in it that indicated that at my height and body frame I was supposed to be between 105-115 pounds and at the time I weighed 124 pounds. I asked my brothers who were 14 and 12 years old at that time, if I was fat to them. They both said "you could lose a little" and started laughing. So I decided I needed to lose weight. I started to run for an hour and exercise excessively after school every day. I told my grandmother that I wanted to drop a few pounds and wanted to stop eating breakfast for a while and she didn't want me to, but said okay as long as I was eating lunch. I got free lunch at school so I sold my lunch card to someone who paid full price for lunch. When my grandmother would make me eat dinner I would go in the bathroom and make myself regurgitate. I was dropping the weight rapidly, my clothes were getting loose and my friends and teachers were asking me why I was losing weight when I was already skinny. At that point, every time I looked in the mirror my image was huge to me. I fainted as I was walking to class one day and woke up in an ambulance. When we got to the hospital they told my grandmother and my mother that I was malnourished and I weighed 96 lbs. I stayed in the hospital for three days with a bland diet of baby food and had to attend outpatient counseling for a diagnosis of anorexia and bulimia nervosa. My grandmother was so hurt and thought it was her lack of supervision that had caused this to happen. She would not allow me to close the door to the bathroom or came in with me to ensure that I did not make myself throw-up.

My anorexia and bulimia continued through college, marriage, and my first pregnancy. When I found out I was pregnant with my first son, I was going on my third month of pregnancy. I did not know I was pregnant because I had lost my menstrual cycle due to my disorders. When I started to gain weight instead of viewing it as an effect of pregnancy I was determined to not get fat and not gain more than 10 pounds. When I met that mark; I started to make myself throw-up. I went for checkups and had dropped weight and the doctor would do an ultrasound each time to ensure my baby was alright. I had two admissions to the hospital due to being dehydrated. My mother and sister came to visit me in Georgia while in the hospital and told me that I had to stop and even threatened to take my baby once born. My husband at the time begged me to stop. My son was born on December 25, 1991 and he was 21inches long and weighed 5.2 pounds at birth. He was full-term but malnourished and had to have an IV attached to him immediately, as did I. I couldn't even breastfeed him. I was so ashamed and hurt because I loved him more than anything-yet I had harmed my baby. He looked like a twig. I begged God to please let me keep my precious Christmas gift and promised Him that I would stop harming myself. He answered my prayer.

I finally was honest with myself and admitted I had a problem. I had to unlearn the behaviors that had become way of life. I sought out professional help from a Psychologist, who specialized in eating disorders and we developed a treatment plan which included individual and group therapy, nutritional and family counseling. We discussed the root causes of my problem and the triggers that lead to the repeat behaviors. Since my triggers were my beliefs of what was a "perfect, beautiful" body image; my therapist wanted me to avoid mirrors, scales, and fashion magazines during my first few months of therapy to aid in combating my disorder. We discussed healthy weight and nutrition so that I could learn that food nourished my body. I had to maintain a food diary. If my weight needed to be monitored I had to leave it up to my doctor. He wanted me to pamper myself with things like getting my hair and nails done, go to movies, read a book, and burn scented candles while taking a bath, during housework, and cooking. None of this was easy, old habits are hard to break, but I stuck with my treatment plan.

I overcame. I started to speak to groups of teenage girls about the disorder. I had another pregnancy 5 years later. I did not turn to my old ways and had a healthier pregnancy. I even had a 30+ pound weight gain over a three year period, but I lost the weight and bodyfat through eating properly and working out with a personal trainer. I am now a certified personal trainer and training for my first fitness competition. If God can restore me from one of the roughest patches of my life he can do the same for others regardless of their anorexia and bulimia or obesity related issues. There's no scale God can't move in the right direction.

Elverna Cain

Day 7: Treat the source not the symptom

Scripture Meditation: 2 Corinthians 10: 7 You are looking at things as they are outwardly. If anyone is confident in himself that he is Christ's, let him consider this again within himself, that just as he is Christ's, so also are we.

Most people are incapable of fully compartmentalizing their lives, so weight and body issues aren't limited to the physical. There's a connection to the mental and even spiritual. To treat your weight issue solely with exercise and nutrition negates a significant part of your being that is pivotal for success. The scale doesn't reflect depression, insecurities, low self-esteem, anger, disappointment, or even hurt. Weight is often a byproduct of these issues. To address your weight without looking deeper places a temporary tourniquet on a wound that requires surgery.

Martin Luther King Jr. said, "In a real sense all life is inter-related. All men are caught in an inescapable network of mutuality, tied in a single garment of destiny. Whatever affects one directly, affects all indirectly. I can never be what I ought to be until you are what you ought to be, and you can never be what you ought to be until I am what I ought to be. This is the inter-related structure of reality."

Although he is referring to interpersonal relationships the same can be said within the individual. We are each comprised of physical, spiritual, and mental parts. "Whatever affects one directly, affects all indirectly." Don't simply look at your dress size, blood pressure levels, or the weight on the scale. Dig deeper than the surface level. Go further than the superficial and allow God to reveal the true strongholds in your life.

1 Sam 16:7 But the LORD said to Samuel, "Do not look at his appearance or at the height of his stature, because I have rejected him; for God sees not as man sees, for man looks at the outward appearance, but the LORD looks at the heart." The reason the United States of America has an obesity issue is not due to overeating and lack of exercise; it's due to a misdiagnosis. God looks at the heart, at the core of our being to find our issues while we simply treat the symptoms.

Meditation Questions: Do you truly have a weight issue or is the true issue being masked by the extra pounds?

Which of the three (mental, spiritual, and physical) tends to be neglected more than others in your life?

Practical Solutions: Begin spending 15 minutes with God daily. Don't focus on your weight or physical appearance. Focus on God through reading of scripture, praise and worshipping and allow him to reveal to you the true root of your weight issue and how He wants to bring wholeness and healing.

Notes

_____

_____

_____

_____

_____

_____

_____

_____

_____

_____

_____

Day 7 Diet: (Eat every 2 hours)

- 1 to 1.5 gallons of water

- 1st Meal:

  o 1 bowl of cherries o 2 mandarins oranges o Grapefruit o 2plums

- 2nd Meal:

  o 2 cups of Broccoli, 1 cup cherry tomatoes, 1 yellow bell pepper (sliced), garlic powder, chili powder, and black pepper for taste. Drizzle with olive oil and Bake @ 400 for 20 mins

- 3rd Meal:

  o 2 cups of Kale, ½ onion (chopped), 2 cloves of garlic (minced), 1 can of Cannellini Beans (rinsed and Drained), 4 cups of Low-Sodium Chicken Broth, black pepper for taste. Sautee onion and garlic in pan until tender. Add Kale. Toss until wilted. Add beans and chicken broth. Reduce heat and let simmer for 15 mins.

- 4th Meal:

  o 1 grape fruit o ¼ cup of blueberries o 1 orange o 1 banana o 2 ounces of carrots

- 5th Meal:

  o 1 White Onion (chopped), 2cloves garlic (minced), 2 Cups of Corn, 2 Large Zucchini (chopped) black pepper to taste. Sautee onion and garlic in olive oil until soft. Add corn and zucchini. Let simmer until tender-crisp. Add pepper for taste.

  o ½ cup of brown rice

- 6th Meal:

- 1 Grapefruit (pealed and separated), 2 mandarin oranges (peeled and separated), ½ cup dried Raspberries, ¼ cup of sliced almonds, 2 cups of Spinach leaves and 2-3 tbsp. Raspberry Fat Free Vinaigrette

- 7th Meal:

    - 2 Medium Red Bell Pepper(halved and cleaned out), ½ onion (chopped and sautéed), 1 cup frozen corn, 1can of Black Beans (drained and rinsed), 1 Garlic Clove (minced) 1 tsp. olive oil, ½ tsp. cayenne pepper, ½ tsp Cumin. Mix Corn, Beans, and onion. Drizzle oil, cayenne pepper, and cumin over vegetables. Toss until fully coated. Fill Bell Pepper halves with mixture. Place on cookie sheet and bake 8-10 mins.

- 8th Meal:

    - 2slices of watermelon o 1 apple o 1 orange o 1 pear

I'd tell myself that I was overweight because I worked these super busy twelve hour night shifts, eating from vending machines, sleeping my days away and that I had no time to exercise. Once the husband and children came along, my rationale turned to the fact that with each pregnancy came additional pounds that I just never shed. There has never been a shortage of excuses for my obesity.

In January 2000, I realized that my family reunion was scheduled for that summer. I was over 200 pounds feeling embarrassed about my appearance and contemplating not attending. I recall my self-esteem plummeting. I also became a pretty convincing actress who was able to mask the insecurities about my size by wearing oversized clothing in an attempt to hide my huge abdomen and dimpled thighs. This led me to devise a plan to shed as much weigh as possible before the event. I seriously engaged in the L.A. Weight Loss program and lost around 60 pounds in 5 months. I remember feeling proud of myself for that accomplishment but it was not truly a success because by the end of 2001 I had gained every ounce back.

Over the years since then I have participated in other weight loss options such as Weight Watcher, Atkins and calorie count diets with the yo-yo effect occurring. You know the dreadful cycle of losing weight and gaining it back repeatedly but never maintaining a healthy weight. By 2010 I weighed over 214 pounds.

Having a clinical background makes me fully aware of the high risk for long term complications related to being obese and having an unhealthy lifestyle such as diabetes, hypertension, heart disease, high cholesterol, and other chronic health conditions. I even hypocritically educate clients about these very issues on a daily basis. These types of consequences became personal for me in April 2014 when I was diagnosed with type 2 diabetes and hypertension. My doctor prescribed medications for both conditions. God knows my voice well but He must have been tired of hearing it at that time because I petitioned Him so much for discipline, direction, and healing. I began making healthier food selections on my own most of the time; as well as, I started walking with a little weight loss but there was no great improvement noted. In June of this year, I saw a post on face book from Ian Buchanan about a transformation program and I contacted him. I joined the program with a goal of getting my lab work within normal ranges and being considered controlled with the diabetes and hypertension. I praise God daily for answering my prayers, in His own time, because through the process I became disciplined and patient. I learned ways to become physically active and be able to make it a part of my daily routine for the rest of my life. I gained the knowledge of proper meal planning that has resulted in completely normal follow up lab work. Through the process I was provided a network of support from others involved in the transformation and a trainer who sincerely cares about others. I have been taken off of medications for the chronic conditions and oh yes- I lost weight.

I charge anyone who is struggling right now with obesity and has a desire for change to consult the Lord for guidance and utilize a reputable program such as the transformation process at D 180 fitness to assist them in accomplishing their goals. After doing so, I can say that I am a better wife, mother, grandmother, daughter, friend, servant...just all around a better me.

Berneda Thompson

Day 8: Making yourself a priority

Scripture Meditation: Proverbs 19:8 He who gets wisdom loves his own soul; He who keeps understanding will find good.

Making ourselves a priority is often times the hardest task to achieve. We're literally pulled in dozens of different directions each with valid significance worthy of our attention. Children, a spouse, work, finances, and church demand our consideration making our desires and even needs a fleeting longing. When you board an airplane no matter how frequently you fly the flight attendants remind you in the case of an emergency the oxygen masks will be released and to always place your mask on first before assisting another passenger.

Why would such a selfish act be a staple command before each plane leaves the runway? Because Delta, Southwest and the dozens of other airlines in the world realize that when you are at your best, then you can assist others to reach their best. Taking care of yourself and obtaining a level of health sustainable for a long life isn't selfish; it's one of the greatest demonstrations of love possible.

"…And when we let our own light shine, we unconsciously give other people permission to do the same. As we are liberated from our own fear, our presence automatically liberates others." God has called each of us to greatness. To be the best version of ourselves possible and that calling is unobtainable when the weight of our weight is tied around our necks.

In order to be selfless you need to be selfish when it comes to your overall health and wellness: mental, physical and spiritual.

If you love your spouse, child, family the best way to demonstrate that is to be present and full of life. It seems a simple enough feat to accomplish but the combination of poor eating habits and lack of exercise has challenged the notion of a long life. Make yourself a priority.

Meditation Questions: Are you giving a certain person or occupation a significant amount of your energy and time at the risk of your personal health?

Do you have moments throughout the week designated for you to focus on the areas of your life that require immediate attention?

Practical Solutions: Begin setting a daily or weekly schedule which includes time for you. Time to exercise, seek God, eat correctly, and to have alone time to unwind. Treat these items on your list with the same respect as your job, your children's extracurricular activities, and your own extracurricular responsibilities. Do not cancel unless its an emergency. Take the time to make you a priority.

Notes

_____

_____

_____

_____

_____

_____

_____

_____

_____

_____

_____

Day 8 Diet: (Eat every 2 hours)

- 1 to 1.5 gallons of water

- 1st Meal:

    o 1 bowl of cherries o 2 mandarins oranges o Grapefruit o
       2plums

- 2nd Meal:

    o 2 cups of Broccoli, 1 cup cherry tomatoes, 1 yellow bell
       pepper (sliced), garlic powder, chili powder, and black
       pepper for taste. Drizzle with olive oil and Bake @ 400 for
       20 mins

- 3rd Meal:

    o 2 cups of Kale, ½ onion(chopped), 2 cloves of garlic
       (minced), 1 can of Cannellini Beans (rinsed and Drained),
       4 cups of Low-Sodium Chicken Broth, black pepper for
       taste. Sautee onion and garlic in pan until tender. Add
       Kale. Toss until wilted. Add beans and chicken broth.
       Reduce heat and let simmer for 15 mins.

- 4th Meal:

    o 1 grape fruit o ¼ cup of blueberries o 1 orange o 1 banana
       o 2 ounces of carrots

- 5th Meal:

    o 1 White Onion (chopped), 2cloves garlic (minced), 2 Cups
       of Corn, 2 Large Zucchini (chopped) black pepper to taste.
       Sautee onion and garlic in olive oil until soft. Add corn
       and zucchini. Let simmer until tender-crisp. Add pepper
       for taste.

    o ½ cup of brown rice

- 6th Meal:

- o 1 Grapefruit (pealed and separated), 2 mandarin oranges (peeled and separated), ½ cup dried Raspberries,¼ cup of sliced almonds, 2 cups of Spinach leaves and 2-3 tbsp. Raspberry Fat Free Vinaigrette

- 7th Meal:

  - o 2 Medium Red Bell Pepper(halved and cleaned out), ½ onion (chopped and sautéed), 1 cup frozen corn, 1can of Black Beans (drained and rinsed), 1 Garlic Clove (minced) 1 tsp. olive oil, ½ tsp. cayenne pepper, ½ tsp Cumin. Mix Corn, Beans, and onion. Drizzle oil, cayenne pepper, and cumin over vegetables. Toss until fully coated. Fill Bell Pepper halves with mixture. Place on cookie sheet and bake 8-10 mins.

- 8th Meal:

  - o 2 slices of watermelon o 1 apple o 1 orange o 1 pear

I can honestly say that at the age of 27, I finally love myself. For years I struggled with being insecure about my body, hiding beneath layers of clothing, and shying away from cameras. I cringed when I got out of the shower in front of the mirror and made a b-line straight for the bedroom. The image I saw was not me. My self-esteem was at an all-time low. How did I let this happen? How did I get so far gone? I weighed more at that point, than I did when I was 9 months pregnant with my son. I remember having pity parties and allowing the depression to take over. I turned to food for comfort and the numbers on the scale continued to climb. I tried to diet and exercise, but things kept coming up. Crazy work schedule, juggling my son, financial issues, exhaustion, house duties… the list went on and on. It wasn't until 2011, that I made a promise to myself to focus on me. I realized that I had to get myself together. If not for my own sake, then for my son's sake.

Things slowly started to fall into place, but getting in shape proved to be the hardest. I tried several different gyms but ended up feeling like I didn't belong. I tried doing it on my own, but I couldn't stay committed. Frustrated and discouraged, I refused to give up. A friend invited me to the fitness studio where she was a member and I agreed to try it. What did I have to lose-other than my thunder thighs and bulging mid-section? Visiting D180Fitness, was the best decision I ever made and marked a turning point in my life. Although I thought I was going to die that day, and the next, and the day after that, I continued to go. I didn't care about not having the nicest workout clothes, being the last person to finish a circuit, or looking a hot sweaty mess at the end of class. The fact of the matter was that I was doing something. Yes, the classes were tough and took everything I had to make it through, but I left feeling like a champion. I never gave up. I learned how to eat healthy and eventually got the guts to incorporate weight training. I was on a mission and nothing could stand in my way. Every pound, inch, and percentage of body fat lost was a victory. My clothes began to fit differently, people began to notice the physical changes, and I began to feel better about myself.

Fast forward two years and I have lost a total of 55 pounds, over 10% body fat, participated in my first fitness competition, and I finally love the skin I'm in. It took a lot of hard work and dedication. There were so many times that I wanted to quit, but I didn't. I have truly transformed my body and in doing so I have transformed my life. I have my confidence and self-esteem back. I am, a better me.

Nikita Mewborn

Day 9: Choose Wisely: Fight or Flight

Scripture Meditation: 1 John 4:4 You are from God, little children, and have overcome them; because greater is He who is in you than he who is in the world.

The human body has two natural responses to danger: Fight or Flight. One prepares to stand its ground in readiness for an attack and will to do whatever is necessary to triumph; while the other surveys the scene for every possible exit. It's important to grasp that these two responses aren't limited to dangerous situations. Fight or flight is a typical response to other life issues such as disagreements, anxiety, frustrations, disappointments, or feelings of helplessness.

When it comes to your fitness journey regardless of your struggle (obesity, anorexia, bulimia, or anything in between) you make the daily decision to fight or flight.

Flight: Frustrated and give up on your diet.

Fight: Exercise after a long grueling day at the office.

Fight: Cooking a healthy meal versus ordering pizza.

The good news is that although these responses are natural reactions they can also be learned behaviors when faced with difficulties. Each day you chose to abstain from temptations, exercise regardless of how you feel, and make healthy life altering decisions you increase your body's tendency to fight. The problem is that we have a generation of men and women who are intimidated to struggle, grind, wrestle, and fight for what is worthwhile. Fleeing takes less effort, less short-term pain, and requires less of an emotional investment. But no battle is ever won with your back to the enemy.

If you're tired of failing, tired of fleeing from the adversary of weight, stop running and rely on the strength of Christ which lies within you, until you are strong enough in spirit, mind and body to claim victory.

"You block your dream when you allow your fear to grow bigger than your faith" (J.P. Stovall)

Meditation Questions: Are you truly willing to stop running from your battle with weight?

What actions can you take to begin fighting versus fleeing?

Practical Solutions: For the next week write down each time you give in to a temptation to eat incorrectly or urge to not exercise. Write down all the feelings associated with the decision made. Also write down each time you did not give in to a temptation to eat incorrectly or urge to not exercise. Write down all the feelings associated with this decision made.

Which decision left you feeling better about yourself?

Notes

_____

_____

_____

_____

_____

_____

_____

_____

_____

_____

_____

Day 9 Diet: (Eat every 2 hours)

- 1 to 1.5 gallons of water

- 1st Meal:

  o 1 Apple (chopped), 1 cup strawberries (halved), 1 Pear (chopped) ½ cup of blueberries. 1 banana (chopped) 1tbsp. honey, 1tsp. Cinnamon. Combine fruit. Drizzle with honey and Cinnamon.

- 2nd Meal:

  o 4 Small Yellow Tomatoes (halved) 4 Small Red Vine Tomatoes(halved) 2 tsp. olive oil, ½ tsp. lemon pepper. 2 tbsp. of Balsamic Vinaigrette. In a bowl toss tomatoes in olive oil. Lay on cookie sheet (seed side up),sprinkle with lemon pepper. Broil in oven until slightly browned. Remove from oven and drizzle with Vinaigrette.

- 3rd Meal:

  o 1 cup Brown Rice (cooked and cooled), 1 Can of Cannellini Beans (Rinsed and Drained), 1/4 cup chopped red onion, 1/4 cup sliced fresh mushrooms, 1/4 cup bite-size broccoli florets, 1/4 cup chopped green and red bell pepper (chopped), ¼ tsp. black pepper, 2 tbsp. Fat Free Italian Dressing. Combine Rice, Beans, and vegetables in a bowl. Drizzle with dressing and toss.

- 4th Meal:

  o 2 Apples (sliced),2 Pears (sliced) 2 Plums (Sliced) ½ cup dried cranberries. 1 tsp. olive oil. 2tbsp. Honey. Spread onto cookie sheet. Drizzle with olive oil and honey

- 5th Meal:

  o 3 Carrots (Julienned), 3 Yellow Squash(Julienned) 3 Zucchini (Julienned) 3 cloves of garlic (minced) ½ white onion(chopped) ½ cup of cherry tomatoes (halved) black pepper to taste. Sautee onion and garlic until soft. Add carrots, squash and zucchini. Cook until al dente. Toss in tomatoes and season with black pepper

- 6th Meal:

  - ½ cup sliced Strawberries, 2 mandarin oranges (peeled and separated), ¼ cup of Blueberries, ¼ cup of sliced almonds,2 cups of Spinach leaves and 2-3 tbsp. Raspberry Fat Free Vinaigrette

- 7th Meal:

  - 3 cups black-eyed peas o 1 cup diced red bell pepper o ½ cup diced onion o 2 cup vegetable broth o ¼ ground red pepper o ½ teaspoon of black pepper

- 8th Meal:

  - 1bowl of cherries o 2 mandarin oranges o ½ Grapefruit

I am a nationally qualified NPC men's physique competitor. I am a certified personal trainer, and have been for several years and I can honestly say, I LOVE FITNESS! There was a time when none of the things above described me; I was in a dark place physically, emotionally, and mentally. In 2011, right after I was married, like many others I got to my heaviest weight ever! I was 221 pounds and I hated how I look and more importantly how I felt. I worked a very stressful job with long hours and lived a sedentary lifestyle. The stress of the new marriage, the job, and finances left me feeling depressed and undesirable. I had received a degree in Exercise Science and I knew a lot about exercise and fitness, but I was not applying any of my knowledge. I basically allowed life and its circumstances to beat me down.

On May 1st, 2012 I was terminated from my job and in hindsite, being fired was one of the best things that happened to me! As I began to search for employment, I made two promises to myself: That I would take my health back and that I would help others do the same. Later that year I got my personal training certification up to date and found employment working in corporate fitness. I also began to lose weight, and boy did it feel great! I could finally take my shirt off at the beach again. I felt more pride in myself and the relationship with my wife grew stronger, not because I looked better, but because I felt better and was able to show her much more love.

In 2013, I continued to work hard in the gym to lose weight, but something happened. I plateaued, and it seemed that nothing I did would get that extra fat off of me. I wanted to be in the best shape of my life, so I decided I would enter a fitness competition.

On January 8th, 2014 I started to prepare for my first physique competition. I had no idea what to think, but I was determined to do it. Over the three plus months I would go hard as I could until I reached my goal. There were days I was tired and would get home and literally pass out! There were days when my food tasted terrible and I wanted to "cheat," but I knew one cheat could lead to several. There were days when my wife hated to be around me because my attitude was terrible! (Those were probably the no carbs days.) Though I had my own personal doubts and personal obstacles to overcome, one thing remained the same: I kept pushing! Every week that I saw improvement in my physique made me want to work that much harder!

As my name was called at my first bodybuilding competition on April 10th, 2014, I felt a sense of pride, joy, and accomplishment. Not only did I reach my goal, but I was truly in the best physical and emotional shape in my life!

Julius Miles

Day 10: Enter the Race

Scripture Meditation: 1 Corinthians 9:24 Do you not know that in a race all the runners run, but only one gets the prize? Run in such a way as to get the prize.

During my senior year of high school I battled ongoing knee issues and my track coach became frustrated with my performances. One day he pulled me aside after practice and said, "Look I know you're hurt, I know you're running in pain. I'm not asking you to win; I'm not asking you to break any records; I'm just asking you to compete. When you step on the track I want you to run as fast, as hard, and as long as you possibly can. I'm not asking you to win; I'm just asking you to compete." Sometimes the formula for success can be broken down to simply showing up and entering the race.

Realistically you're going to fail on occasion. Meals won't be prepared in time, your cravings for fast food will win, the cold weather will be your excuse for not exercising, and you may simply grow weary of the healthy lifestyle every so often. This does not define you. The fact that you had the courage and drive to enter the race and simply compete does.

The amazing thing about our relationship with God is that no matter how often we fall short of the mark he graciously gives us second opportunities to pass the same test we just failed. Hopefully you see the similarity with your personal fitness journey. No matter how badly you eat, how many workouts you miss, or how discouraged you've been; tomorrow is a new day and new opportunity to pass the same test you just failed.

Something amazing happens when you demonstrate the willingness to simply compete. When you toe the starting line with all your weaknesses, your insecurities, your unbridled self-discipline, and even lack of knowledge ready to run the race the best you can., God comes alongside you, matching you stride for stride and perfects the areas in which your human imperfections boldly shine through.

The resurrection power of Christ has the power to speak to every situation in your life once viewed as dead and hopeless. Rely on his word, his promises, and support in every area of life including your weight. Toe the line. Run the race. Compete.

Meditation Questions: Are you relying on the power of God to overcome your weight issues or attempting to achieve success with your own abilities?

Do you truly believe that God has the ability to deliver you from the struggle and even strongholds you have when it comes to your weight?

Practical Solutions: Create a list of all the miracles you personally know Jesus has done in the bible. Now create a second list of the miracles he's performed in your life. Use these lists to strengthen your resolve in regards to God's ability to perform another in regards to your fitness journey.

Break each of your exercise sessions up in small segments. Instead of one consistent hour workout for 10 minutes and allow yourself a 2-3 minute break before exercising for another 10 minutes.

Notes

_____

_____

_____

_____

_____

_____

_____

_____

_____

Day 10 Diet: (Eat every 2 hours)

- 1 to 1.5 gallons of water

- 1stMeal:

  o 1 Apple (chopped), 1 cup strawberries (halved), 1 Pear (chopped) ½ cup of blueberries. 1 banana (chopped) 1tbsp. honey, 1tsp. Cinnamon. Combine fruit. Drizzle with honey and Cinnamon.

- 2ndMeal:

  o 4 Small Yellow Tomatoes (halved) 4 Small Red Vine Tomatoes(halved) 2 tsp. olive oil, ½ tsp. lemon pepper. 2 tbsp. of Balsamic Vinaigrette. In a bowl toss tomatoes in olive oil. Lay on cookie sheet (seed side up),sprinkle with lemon pepper. Broil in oven until slightly browned. Remove from oven and drizzle with Vinaigrette.

- 3rd Meal:

  o 1 cup Brown Rice (cooked and cooled), 1 Can of Cannellini Beans (Rinsed and Drained), 1/4 cup chopped red onion, 1/4 cup sliced fresh mushrooms, 1/4 cup bite-size broccoli florets, 1/4 cup chopped green and red bell pepper (chopped), ¼ tsp. black pepper, 2 tbsp. Fat Free Italian Dressing. Combine Rice, Beans, and vegetables in a bowl. Drizzle with dressing and toss.

- 4th Meal:

  o 2 Apples (sliced),2 Pears (sliced) 2 Plums (Sliced) ½ cup dried cranberries. 1 tsp. olive oil. 2tbsp. Honey. Spread onto cookie sheet. Drizzle with olive oil and honey

- 5th Meal:

  o 3 Carrots (Julienned), 3 Yellow Squash(Julienned) 3 Zucchini (Julienned) 3 cloves of garlic (minced) ½ white onion(chopped) ½ cup of cherry tomatoes (halved) black pepper to taste. Sautee onion and garlic until soft. Add carrots, squash and zucchini. Cook until al dente.Toss in tomatoes and season with black pepper

- 6th Meal:

  - ½ cup sliced Strawberries, 2 mandarin oranges (peeled and separated), ¼ cup of Blueberries, ¼ cup of sliced almonds,2 cups of Spinach leaves and 2-3 tbsp. Raspberry Fat Free Vinaigrette

- 7th Meal:

  - 3 cups black-eyed peas o 1 cup diced red bell pepper o ½ cup diced onion o 2 cup vegetable broth o ¼ ground red pepper o ½ teaspoon of black pepper

- 8th Meal:

  - 1bowl of cherries o 2 mandarin oranges o ½ Grapefruit

I endured a lot of struggles at an early age brought on from being bullied, which was a normal affliction growing up in the community I came from. I was criticized and harassed a lot as a child; the tougher kids took advantage of my shyness. My family lived in poverty and my father was nonexistent in my life. Other kids attitudes towards me made me feel alienated and ostracized. I had no sense of belonging and only wanted to be accepted and respected. I eventually connected with negative influences and bad crowds to fit in. This is when I realized by the examples of my buddies at the time that if I committed crimes and acted out I could get some sort of recognition, respect and acceptance within my world. I started committing crimes in order to receive the things that people respected in my culture: drugs, cars, money of course and eventually prestige. I've been shot, stabbed, dragged by a car and eventually ended up in jail on numerous occasions.

One thing I've realized through my 18 years of incarceration is that God can take a curse and turn it into a blessing. As ironic as it sounds prison is where I achieved my freedom. Mentally I was handcuffed to a mindset cultivated in the hood and physically I entered prison at the heaviest I'd ever been. The world has a tendency to give up on people who make mistakes but God remains constant and continued to work from the inside out in my life. My relationship with God became stronger as I began to seek him daily and through his direction I discovered a healthy outlet to dealing with frustration, anger, and disappointment. Exercise became my saving grace mentally and physically. I found myself at the healthiest and leanest point of my life but even more importantly I found my passion and calling.

After being released from jail I continued my personal pursuits of health and fitness and joined D180Fitness. I was asked by the owner, "what is your 5 year plan?" My response was I always wanted to teach physical fitness since I loved working out and eventually open up my own gym. I started studying as a student of fitness and I've recently obtained my certification as a personal trainer. Now I spend my days helping others rediscover themselves through health and fitness and allowing God to transform them from the inside out and reviving their inner strength.

God is in the business of restoring the damaged. When surrendered to God, lives, bodies, mental states, or even families can all be resurrected. If he did it for me, he can do it for you.

Joe Bond

Join the D180Fitness Family by visiting www.d180fitness.com for encouragement, support and fitness tips. Use the password, "fit4life" for an $11 per month membership.